GW00374597

Roman Fortifications on the 'Saxon Shore'

Stephen Johnson

London
Her Majesty's Stationery Office

ACKNOWLEDGEMENTS

The Department of the Environment is grateful to the following authorities for permission to reproduce illustrations:

Schleswig-Holstein Landesmuseum for the Nydam ship (p.4)

Norfolk Archaeological Unit for the air view of Brancaster Fort (p.8)

University of Cambridge Committee for Aerial Photography for the view of Lympne (p.11) and Bradwell (p.19)

The British Museum for the Arras medallion and the coins of Carausius and Allectus (pp.12, 13, 16)

The Bodleian Library for the cover picture: the Insignia of the Count of the Saxon Shore

© Crown Copyright 1977
First published 1977

ISBN 0 11 670340 7

Cover: Insignia of the Count of the Saxon Shore from the copy of the *Notitia Dignitatum* in the Bodleian Library.

The direction of Saxon raiding

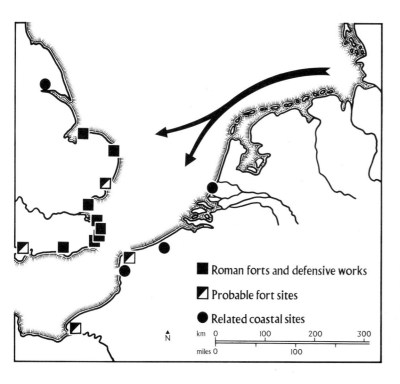

■ Roman forts and defensive works

◨ Probable fort sites

● Related coastal sites

N

km 0   100   200   300

miles 0   100

F OR NEARLY FOUR HUNDRED YEARS, from AD 43 until about AD 410, Britain was part of the Roman Empire. During such a long period there were phases of growth and decline, contentment and rebellion, peace and war. By and large, the southern parts of Britain were relatively undisturbed throughout the Roman period, whereas the north was a military area, always garrisoned by army units in their grim forts, on continual watch to control the border traffic between the non-Romans in the southern parts of Scotland and their neighbours who lived on the Roman side of the frontier formed by Hadrian's Wall.

The situation on the northern frontier was not always tense, nor was there always peace in the south. The remains of large, powerfully constructed Roman forts which line the southern and eastern coastlines – the 'Saxon Shore' – suggest that even here the Romans were under hostile pressure. These forts, built in a solid masonry which has stood against the elements for seventeen centuries, are eloquent testimony that the south-eastern tip of Britain became an area of Roman military concern. But when was its peace disturbed, and from which direction did the threat come?

The late third century was a time of crisis for much of the western half of the Roman empire. Barbarian tribesmen, whose homes lay beyond the borders of the

3

The Nydam ship, a Saxon warship of about AD 400 found preserved in marshes on the borders of Denmark and Germany. It was crammed with weapons and, though powered only by oars, must have been the sort of ship in which Saxons menaced coasts of Britain

Roman world, swept down into the unsuspecting and largely undefended areas of central Gaul, looting and pillaging as they went. Territory in Germany which the Romans had controlled was now abandoned: all over the empire new forts went up and new walls were built to defend the towns and cities.

The invaders were Alemanni, Franks and Saxons, who plundered and harassed not only the inland areas of central and western Gaul, but also the low-lying coastal zones, among them the channel coasts of Gaul and Britain. The sea-borne Saxons were the raiders most feared: their mobility enabled them to strike suddenly and ruthlessly. Rome's solution to similar problems elsewhere was to retreat inside well-defined and more easily defensible natural boundaries: but here, on the exposed eastern coasts of Britain, there was no such barrier to raise against the longships of the Saxon, sweeping down the coasts from the base of the Danish peninsula.

What, then, was the 'Saxon Shore'? It was a series of fortifications designed to curb the activities of Saxon pirates in the Channel and the North Sea areas. In their longships, the Saxons were extremely mobile: they could slip, under cover of rough weather or even darkness, up the river estuaries and creeks, surprising rich areas sometimes deep inland. Roman tactics demanded that as many as possible of the obvious inlets should be sealed off, thus denying the Saxons access to the areas deeper inland. The chain of coastal fortifications was built at the mouths of the main rivers; they contained troops to contest any attempted landing by the pirates, and a fleet to give chase once their presence had been discovered.

The name 'Saxon Shore' comes down to us from the *Notitia Dignitatum*, a list of late Roman date (about AD 400) which gives in full detail a review of the commands and postings of all the troops in the Roman world, including Britain. One of its chapters is devoted to the command of the *Comes Litoris Saxonici per Britannias* (the Count of the 'Saxon Shore' in the British provinces), who was in charge of the forts which line the southern and eastern coastlines of Britain. Though the list in the *Notitia* mentions only nine forts, it is possible that in earlier days the Count had more forts under his command, for there are remains or records of at least ten coastal forts in the south-eastern part of Britain, all of which may at some time have formed the defensive chain.

The nine forts which the *Notitia* mentions are given, of course, with their Roman names, so it is not always easy to link up the present-day remains with their original names, but, listed in the order in which they appear in the *Notitia*, the sites are as follows:

Othona	Bradwell
Dubris	Dover
Lemannis	Lympne
Branodunum	Brancaster
Gariannonum	Burgh Castle
Regulbium	Reculver
Rutupiae	Richborough
Anderida (-ita)	Pevensey
Portus Adurni	Portchester or Walton Castle

Some of these names can be seen to correspond quite closely with their Roman originals, and thus are probably accurately identified. A superficial resemblance of Roman and modern names is sometimes misleading, however, for the River Adur, which flows into the sea at Shoreham, was so named by nineteenth-century antiquaries who thought that at its mouth was an ideal spot for the Roman *Portus Adurni* to have lain. Even now, we cannot be sure which fort was *Portus Adurni*: it may have been Portchester, near the entrance to Southampton Water, or Walton Castle, a fort now lost in the sea, but which originally stood near Felixstowe.

The importance of the *Notitia* list in which these names figure is twofold; first, it shows that there was a system of forts under a single commander in Britain. This was a frontier, intended to be as much a barrier against the sea-raiders from the east as was Hadrian's Wall against the northern tribes. Second, the *Notitia* shows that there were originally at least two forts which formed part of the same system in Gaul. Again, only the Roman names of these have been handed down to us, and unfortunately no remains similar to those in Britain have been found with which they can be identified.

The *Notitia*, in chapters other than that which deals with the Saxon Shore, lists a string of names for coastal fortifications in Gaul, extending from the mouth of the Rhine along the northern and western coasts as far as Bordeaux, on the Garonne. The majority of these names are of Roman cities which lay on the coast – places like Nantes, Vannes, Avranches, Coutances and even Rouen (which lay on the Seine, but was apparently still part of the coastal system). These probably represent a very late Roman addition to the defensive screen in the channel, and their garrisoning was probably an emergency measure undertaken in the face of very serious, renewed pressure from the Saxons towards the end of the fourth century. Such forts of

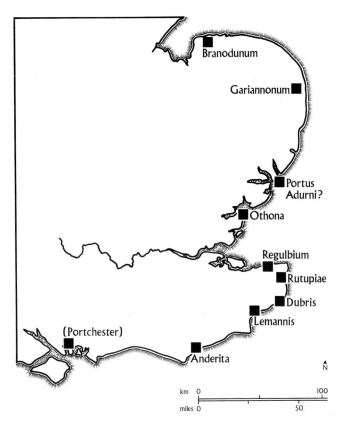

The 'Saxon Shore' forts in Britain

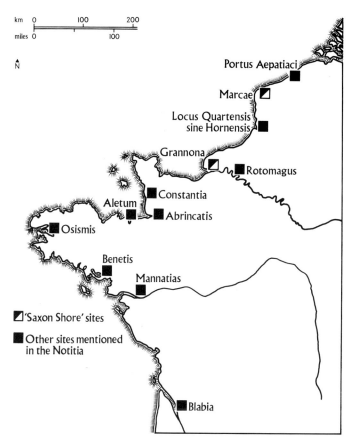

Portus Aepatiaci

Marcae

Locus Quartensis
sine Hornensis

Grannona

Rotomagus

Constantia

Aletum

Abrincatis

Osismis

Benetis

Mannatias

◪ 'Saxon Shore' sites

■ Other sites mentioned
in the Notitia

Blabia

Continental shore-defences

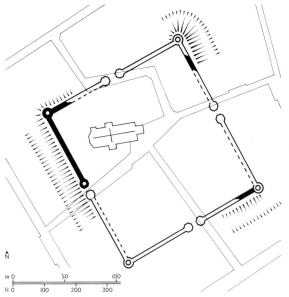

m 0 ... 50 ... 100
ft 0 ... 100 ... 200 ... 300

Plan of the fort discovered in excavation at Oudenburg, near Bruges

purely military origin as there were in Gaul lay in the area more directly opposite Britain, and include sites like Oudenburg in Belgium, where a fort with plan and dimensions remarkably similar to the British 'Saxon Shore' forts has recently been discovered by excavation. The two forts which are described in the *Notitia* as 'on the Saxon Shore' are *Marcae* and *Grannona*, but in the region where they might be expected to have lain, the former near Boulogne, and the latter somewhere near the mouth of the Seine, there have so far been no discoveries of forts of this type.

We do not know at what date this system of forts was called the 'Saxon Shore'. It is not even certain exactly how the name should be applied – whether it implies that the Saxons were settlers or attackers. One of Rome's more successful methods of containing the attacks from barbarian tribesmen was to grant groups of settlers land to farm just within the empire's borders. Thus the settlers gained an interest in the land, and, if needed, could also become mercenary soldiers to help protect their own holdings from attack from outside. Whether the Roman authorities ever gave groups of Saxons land to settle in this way is not certain: there is only slight evidence to suggest that Saxons were present and settling on the eastern coasts of Britain before AD 400. The 'Saxon Shore' forts may have had the double task of repelling the invading tribesmen and watching over the more peaceable settlers. However the name grew up, it is clear from the *Notitia* list that the 'Saxon Shore' was regarded first and foremost as a military frontier; the Saxons were a hostile and savage enemy, a dangerous threat to the peace of the whole empire.

THE HISTORY OF THE COMMAND

There is some indication that bands of raiders had been occasional, if not constant, visitors to Britain's eastern coasts for perhaps the fifty years before the construction of the main series of fortifications in AD 270-285. In response to this earlier threat, a series of harbours down

Brancaster from the air. The levelled ramparts of the fort are visible as a parched mark in the field in the foreground. The further field shows traces of an extra-mural settlement.

Channel coastal defences in the early third century (AD 200-250)

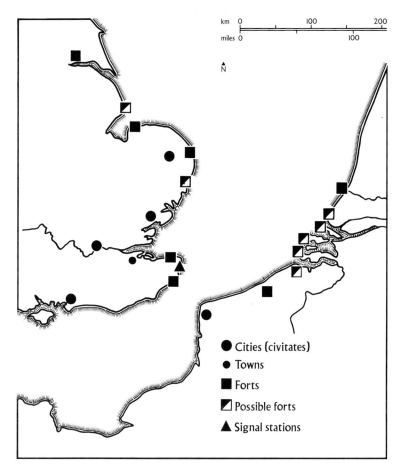

● Cities (civitates)

• Towns

■ Forts

◪ Possible forts

▲ Signal stations

the eastern coast was put on a mobile footing. Sites which were thus pressed into service included Brough-on-Humber, Caister-on-Sea (near Great Yarmouth), and Rochester. There already existed a naval base for the Roman British Fleet (*Classis Britannica*) at Dover, and this was supplemented, in AD 220-230, by the construction of two further forts, Brancaster and Reculver, guarding the Wash and the Thames Estuary. Today, Brancaster fort lies in a field and one can now only pick up the fort's outline in photographs taken when the field was under crop, but at Reculver, where about half of the fort has been washed away by the sea, parts of the ramparts are still visible.

Both of these forts were built in a style that was traditional to Britain: their shape is that of a playing-card – rectangular with rounded corners – and they had internal turrets at the corners and gateways. The walls were slightly thicker than earlier Roman forts in the north, but they were still backed by an earth rampart which gave them an extra solidity and provided sufficient thickness for a fighting platform at the top of the walls.

By the end of the third century, however, these defensive measures were proving inadequate. The Frankish and Saxon pirates who were infesting the seas seem to have tested the resources of the old British Fleet to the utmost: a revitalised fleet and a new system of defence was needed, not only to chase the pirates out of the areas they found so productive, but also to make sure that they stayed out, and ceased to molest the traffic plying its trade between Britain and Gaul.

New forts were therefore added to the two already built: all lay on river estuaries or on other natural harbours, and several had formerly been the sites of

9

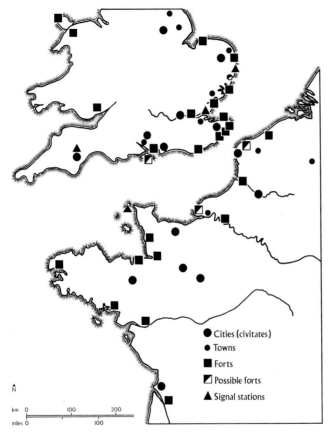

Cities (civitates)

• Towns

■ Forts

◪ Possible forts

▲ Signal stations

N

km 0   100   200

miles 0   100

Roman defences in the channel areas after AD 275

smaller civilian settlements or even earlier fleet-bases. Burgh Castle lay on a tidal estuary of the Wensum or Yare, a river which reached deep into the centre of East Anglia, and on which lay the main port for Caistor-by-Norwich, the capital of the Iceni. Walton Castle, built on a site which had been a small *vicus* (village), guarded the estuaries of three rivers, the Orwell, the Stour and the Deben. Bradwell, also built on an earlier site, protected the Blackwater estuary and the approaches to Colchester in the same way. In Kent, three further forts were added, to increase the defensive force at the Channel straits. The two main ports of entry into Britain, Dover and Richborough, were now fortified with walls of massive late Roman construction. At Dover, the new fort partly overlay the destroyed ruins of the earlier *Classis Britannica* base, and at Richborough the ground was levelled in preparation for construction, even though there had previously been a large triumphal monument recording the conquest of Britain standing proudly on the spot which was to become the centre of the Roman fort. At Lympne, possibly in earlier days a base for the *Classis Britannica*, the remains of another Roman fort are now isolated above the Dymchurch marshes: here, as in many places, the coastline has changed since Roman days, and the fort used to lie on the estuary of a river which reached well inland into the central parts of Kent.

To complete the system at this date, the fort of Portchester was constructed on low ground next to the sea in what is now Portsmouth Harbour. The final fort which is mentioned in the *Notitia* list, Pevensey, was probably built later, in AD 340, to close the wide gap between Lympne and Portchester on the southern coast. Although this site too is now landlocked, it is on a

Lympne fort from the air

slight rise amid flatlands, and would originally have been virtually surrounded by the sea.

It is to the end of the third century, a time roughly contemporary with the construction of these forts, that the story of Carausius, apparently the first commander of the system, belongs. Despite his privileged position as the first to take control of the late Roman channel defensive screen, Carausius would have been unremarkable, and probably unknown to us, were it not for the fact that, basing his power on the fleet and the newly built forts, he laid claim to imperial power. The story, as far as we can piece it together from the various mentions in historical sources, goes like this.

Carausius was of humble origin among the Menapian tribe (who lived in what is now Holland), and was employed in his youth among merchant ships plying their trade between Holland, Britain and the Rhineland area. He was recruited into the Roman army, and in the operations that restored peace to the Roman world after barbarian invasions in Europe (in the AD 260s and 270s) he gained distinction and promotion for bravery. When the channel command was established to control the activities of the Saxon pirates, Carausius, because of his sailing experience, was the obvious choice to prepare the fleet and oversee the working of the defences.

In the meantime, Maximian, under whose generalship Carausius had earlier so distinguished himself, was elevated by Diocletian, then emperor, to be his partner in the imperial command. Carausius was perhaps jealous of Maximian's power, and felt (possibly rightly) that some of it was a result of his own exploits. There was clearly no love lost between these two men, and Maximian, seeking a chance to bring his enemy's downfall, had Carausius summoned on a charge that he was misappropriating the bullion and plunder that he had captured from Saxon pirates. Carausius was a wanted man: the charge was treason, the penalty death.

Forced into open revolt, Carausius adopted a bold plan. He declared himself emperor, claiming equality with Diocletian and Maximian. The fleet and his troops were loyal, and his command stretched over Britain and enough of northern Gaul to make his control of the channel secure. Protected thus by his faithful followers, Carausius was assured of at least temporary safety; other affairs for the moment claimed Maximian's attention, and Carausius's control of the fleet and the channel areas meant that any approach to enforce the imperial ruling was for the moment impossible.

In AD 286 Carausius had declared himself emperor. In the following five years he did much to put the economic stability of Britain back on a sound footing: he issued new coinage with more precious metal content to combat inflation; he ensured the safety of trading with the Continent by his policing of the shipping lanes. But this was not to last. In AD 289-290, Maximian was building a fleet on the Rhine to depose him. The outcome of this expedition was a failure, but further attempts were to follow. In AD 293, by a brilliant tactical stroke, a new general, Constantius, acting for Maximian, took the walls of Boulogne by siege, blocking approach to the walled city by sea with a hastily constructed dam. Carausius's troops, trapped in the citadel, had to surrender: reinforcements could not approach from the sea, and there were insufficient men to risk a pitched battle. The capture of Boulogne virtually assured the success of Maximian's campaigns. Carausius, defeated and partly discredited, returned to Britain, where his former finance minister Allectus,

Portraits of Carausius (above) *and Allectus* (below) *from their coinage*

The Arras medallion portraying the recapture of Britain by Constantius in AD 296. On the right is the walled city of London joyfully receiving the Caesar on horseback.

who was probably responsible for many of the positive achievements of the Carausian régime, engineered his assassination and took power himself.

But Allectus's success was short-lived. A Roman fleet, better prepared and better equipped than the last, moved stealthily on Britain in AD 296. One force landed near the Isle of Wight and headed for London. A pincer movement was aimed to bring a second force up the Thames and into London's harbour. Allectus was trapped in indecision. In a desperate attempt to save London, he was caught and killed, his mercenary troops slaughtered, in a battle near Silchester. Many of his supporters, barbarian troops who were enrolled to supplement the regular units, deserted, and, in a bid to grab what they could from the situation, marched on London intent on pillage and plunder. Constantius himself, in the second fleet, arrived just in time to prevent a disaster: London welcomed him back with open arms (*see* coin on this page).

After Allectus's death, which closed this episode, we hear little more in historical sources about the Channel area. The system of forts built for Carausius was kept unchanged, and the only indication that the frontier line was in effective use is the silence of Roman historians about Saxon attacks. Forts in a style similar to those on the 'Saxon Shore' were built at Cardiff and Lancaster, possibly to meet a growing threat from the Scots in Ireland. In the AD 340s, the emperor Constans visited Britain, hurriedly answering some emergency which may have included trouble on the south-eastern coast. At about this time, Pevensey was added to the system, and a small defended site at Bitterne, now part of Southampton, may also have been built to add to the coastal screen.

The west gate at Pevensey. The main entrance to the Roman fort is protected by this massive pair of bastions

Aerial view of Portchester

In AD 367 came a real crisis. Picts and Scots mounted an attack on Britain from the north, and Saxons simultaneously threatened areas in the South. One general was captured, and another, described by a near-contemporary historian as the 'count of the maritime area' was killed. This count is probably none other than the Count of the Saxon Shore, whose office is listed in the *Notitia*. The situation was soon restored with prompt action by Theodosius, and though raids by Saxons are mentioned ever more frequently in historical sources, there is no further reappearance of the frontier or its commander. By the time of the compilation of the *Notitia* list in AD 395 or thereabouts, the Count is recorded as holding only nine garrisoned forts in Britain alone. By now, this command had been sub-divided, and the forts on the Continent given over to new commanders in Gaul with responsibility for the Belgian coast, and the broad sweep of 'Armorican' coastline, from the Seine to the Garonne.

By the early fifth century, most of Rome's connections with Britain had been severed. The power of Rome was crumbling from pressure by barbarians on many frontiers. Britain, as a province of the Roman empire, was abandoned and left to defend itself as best it could. Deprived of troops who could keep a constant guard, the forts of the Saxon Shore were abandoned: the sites of some were even taken over by Saxons who came in the fifth and sixth centuries to settle on the eastern seaboard. Some decayed, and the stone was carted off elsewhere for use in other buildings. Others formed a convenient site for Saxon monasteries or Norman castles. But, surprisingly (or perhaps as a result), several of them have survived in a remarkable state of preservation. Of the ten forts, four are now

Reverse of a coin of Allectus showing the type of Roman ship in use in Britain

Burgh Castle from the air

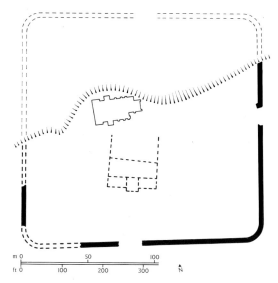

Outline plan of Reculver Roman fort. The building south of the church on the water's edge is the fort's headquarters, known from excavation only.

Reculver Towers, remains of the parish church of Reculver within the Roman fort

Reculver was built earlier than the main series of Saxon Shore forts, and thus it has more affinities with the earlier style of Roman military architecture than with the more massive forts that ringed the south-eastern corner of Britain. In the fort's headquarters building, found to lie in the field immediately south of the towers of the church, fragments of an inscription came to light in 1960: it records the construction of the fort under a third-century consular governor of Britain. This discovery is one of the more important finds from Saxon Shore forts in recent years and helps to show that the development of the defensive system round the channel coast was a gradual process in response to a build-up of Saxon pressure, and not an immediate answer to some swift, surprise attack.

Richborough is perhaps the most important fort of the whole system. About three-quarters of its interior has been totally excavated, and the remains of many periods other than those which belong specifically to the Saxon Shore fort phase have been found there. The walls of the fort, still standing impressively high, were among the latest features built on the site, for Richborough, as one of the main ports of entry into Roman Britain, had a long history, stretching over at least two centuries before there was a need for fortification of the key harbours in the south-east. Although now land-bound, it was a peninsula in Roman times: this held a bridge-head fort in the early stages of the Roman invasion of Britain in AD 43, and later the site was converted into a stores base for the support of Roman troops campaigning in the south and west of Britain.

In the later first and early second century, Richborough settled down to a more peaceful phase of its existence. Centrally in the site, a monument proclaiming the triumph of the Romans over Britain was erected, and shops and houses, warehouses and temples undoubtedly extended well beyond the limits of the site now excavated and on view. The amphitheatre (like the fort, in the guardianship of the Department, although not yet excavated), testifies to a life which had time for entertainment among the business of a thriving port.

Early in the third century, this picture began to change. The central monument, then in disrepair, was patched up and used as a watch-tower. Triple ditches were dug to surround it, converting the centre of the site into a small defended post. More desperate measures were to come, for in about AD 275 the site was levelled and construction of the stone fort began. The walls were massive – 12 feet (3.6 m) thick – and enclosed a rectangular area. At intervals along the walls there were strong, rectangular projecting towers. At the corners, round towers were built and the gates were either simple passageways flanked by a further pair of massive bastions or cunning entrances hidden in one of the rectangular towers. To complete the defences, double ditches surrounded the walls. Tidal action in the former estuary of the River Stour, already cutting close to it in the late Roman period, has undermined the eastern side of the fort, and the east wall together with parts of the two walls adjoining it has now toppled and lies at what was probably sea-level in Roman times.

Inside the fort, the monument had been razed. In its place was built a headquarters-building of stone, but the majority of the inner buildings were of wooden construction and have left no visible trace. These were probably barrack-blocks for the second Legion Augusta, which was stationed here in the fourth century. One building of particular interest, dating from the very latest years of the fort's use, is a church. This, too, was of timber, and all that can now be seen of it is the tiled basin (in the north-west corner of the fort) which was its baptismal font.

Finds from Richborough have long formed one of the most notable collections of Roman material from an excavated site in Britain. Its coin series, unlike that at other sites, shows a marked increase in the number of issues for years following AD 410, traditionally the year in which the Romans left Britain, and therefore the date at which coinage from Roman mints ceased to be in plentiful supply. The astonishing number of these late coins from Richborough indicates that the fort was in use up to and a little after AD 410, and emphasises the importance of the site not only while Britain was a Roman province, but also at a time when her links with Rome were no longer strong.

The exact site of the fort at **Dover** was not confirmed until 1970, when excavation in advance of a new road-scheme located not only the Saxon Shore fort underlying the kernel of the medieval and modern town, but also the remains of an earlier (probably second and third century) fort which housed the sailors of the British Fleet, the Roman *Classis Britannica*. This early fort was rectangular in plan with rounded corners: it was superseded by a strongly built fort of Saxon Shore type with walls more than 6 feet (2 m) thick. This had partly overlain the earlier fort and had one of its sides directly against the estuary of the River Dour, where remains of a Roman quayside had previously been dicovered. The Saxon Shore fort defences were strengthened by a ditch and by externally projecting

The west wall of the fort at Richborough

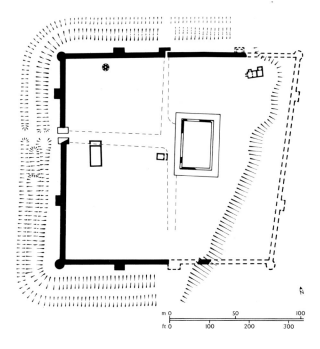

Plan of the late-Roman features at Richborough

semicircular towers. One of the most notable finds at Dover is the remains of a house, contemporary with the early fort, whose walls were decorated with painted wall-plaster. This had been preserved because it was buried by a rampart-bank thrown up behind the Saxon Shore fort wall. Excavations have not, however, revealed the full extent of this late Roman fort; the south and west walls have been located, but most of the excavated areas have been backfilled and are not now on view.

The most prominent Roman monument in Dover is the pharos, standing high above the modern town within the enclave of the Castle. This, originally one of a pair flanking the Dover estuary, will have guided ships into the harbour. Its survival is due to its later use as the tower of the church of St Mary ad Castro, which lies next to it. Less fortunate has been the Bredenstone, its opposite number on the Western Heights. A similar Roman lighthouse, now destroyed, but portrayed on a drawing of the siege of Boulogne in 1544, stood at Boulogne.

Stutfall Castle at **Lympne**, the next Roman fort of the chain, now lies in tumbled fragments at the foot of a slope below the medieval castle at Lympne. The fort lies at the marsh-edge, which, though now silted, was in Roman times part of tidal estuary of the *Lemannis* (River Rother). The fort walls, now very much ruined, lie at crazy angles where landslides have made them slip and fall, but would in Roman times have enclosed an irregular pentagonal area. Though it is difficult now to visualise their original appearance, the walls were thick and strong, in all aspects similar to those of Richborough or Pevensey.

The site has been the subject of only limited exca-

vation. Remains of two internal buildings were revealed and recorded in the mid-nineteenth century, as was the eastern gateway. Re-examination of this in 1976 has led to the reinterpretation of the gate as a single-portalled entrance flanked by semicircular towers.

The walls of the fort at **Pevensey** form a prominent feature of the present village. The main road has had to make a substantial detour to pass round the outside of the fort enclosure. The fort's oval shape makes Pevensey unusual. Apart from Lympne, which was pentagonal, the other Saxon Shore forts are rectangular or quadrilateral in plan. Pevensey takes its oval shape from the knoll that it occupies, in Roman times surrounded by water inlets and marshes.

Prominent round the walls, which still stand up to 30 feet (10 m) high in places are the massive U-shaped external towers. The western gateway, the Roman main entrance, is flanked by a similar pair of bastions, with the actual gate entrance well recessed behind them. The central area of the fort is now pasture, but excavation has shown that there were once Roman timber barrack-blocks with tiled hearths, similar to those at Richborough and possibly Burgh Castle. The walls enclose about 10 acres (4 ha) and thus make Pevensey the largest of the forts: built of limestone, ironstone and tiles, they stand a formidable 12 feet (3.6 m) thick.

The walls originally stood on a framework of large timber baulks in the foundation courses. During the course of centuries, the timber has of course rotted and crumbled to dust, leaving only the chases. In one such hole, underneath one of the towers, a coin dated AD 335

The Pharos, remains of the Roman lighthouse at Dover

was found. This possibly gives a date after which the fort was built and shows that, as well as being the largest and the most irregular of the forts, Pevensey was also the latest of the series.

Here, as at Burgh Castle, the Norman lords found the outer walls suitable for the outer enclosure, or bailey, of their feudal castle. An eleventh-century castle was built within the walls, at the eastern end of the former enclosure.

The last of the forts normally included among those of the Saxon Shore is at **Portchester**, overlooking Portsmouth Harbour. At high tide, the sea washes its walls, because it stands on a slight platform at sea level, partly jutting out into the harbour.

Here, as well, a Norman castle was built in the corner of the fort, but the rectangle of impressive walls, ringed with flanking towers, is Roman in origin; as are the ditches which surround the fort.

The Landgate, through which one enters, is a medieval addition to the circuit: the Roman gates were, like those at Pevensey, recessed a little, and the foundations of a spur wall linking the gate to the main circuit can be seen on the right on entering. The towers, U-shaped and hollow, have probably been partly refaced in medieval times, but still preserve the aspect of the Roman fort as it would originally have been. The enclosing wall has also been narrowed in later times, and its original width would have been about 11 feet (3·3 m).

Excavations at the fort have shown that there were several periods of occupation from the later third century through to the end of the Roman period (AD 275–c.410), but after 367 it seems not to have

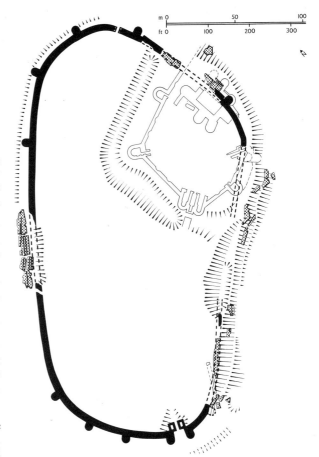

Plan of Pevensey Roman fort (in solid black) and medieval castle

The Watergate at Portchester, on the site of the Roman watergate

been in use by Roman troops. There are some traces of Saxon settlement, perhaps as early as the late fifth century, and the enclosure within the fort walls was in frequent use from then until the construction of the Norman castle by Henry I.

Portchester remained an important royal castle and place of assembly for expeditions, until it gradually lost this function to Portsmouth itself and was abandoned. It was called back into use as a prisoner-of-war camp during the wars of the eighteenth century, down to the Napoleonic period.

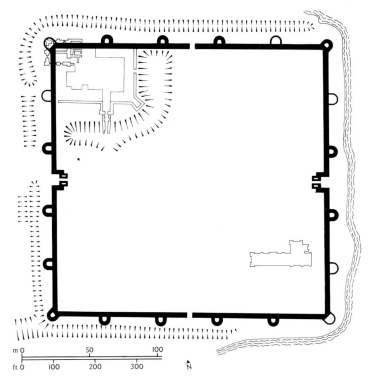

Plan of Portchester Roman fort (in solid black) with the inserted medieval castle and monastic church.